To:

From:

OUTDOOR GRILLING

and barbecue favorites

Printed in the United States of America

ISBN 1-56383-016-7

TABLE OF CONTENTS

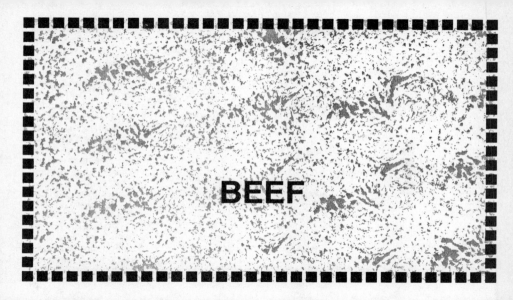

ROUNDUP ROUND STEAK

2 to 3 lb. beef round steak (about 1" thick), chilled
1 C. Chablis wine
½ C. lemon juice
½ C. salad oil
2 tsp. salt
1 tsp. leaf oregano
2 cloves garlic, crushed

Combine wine, lemon juice, oil, salt, oregano and garlic in saucepan. Bring to boil. Reduce heat and simmer 10 minutes. Chill. Score steak on both sides in diamond pattern, about ⅛" deep. Place steak in plastic bag or shallow dish and marinate. Keep in refrigerator 6 to 8 hours. Remove steak from sauce and place on grill. Cook at medium heat 25 to 35 minutes, brushing occasionally.

BIG BEEF SANDWICH

*3 lb. chuck or round steak,
 2" thick
Instant meat tenderizer
½ C. soft butter or margarine*

*2 T. prepared mustard
1 T. prepared horseradish
1 loaf French bread, 18" long
Freshly ground coarse
 pepper*

Slash fat edges of steak. Sprinkle meat tenderizer on steak (according to directions on label). Broil on grill 2" from coals 25 to 30 minutes. Turn often. Do not overcook. Mix butter, mustard and horseradish. Cut bread lengthwise in half. Toast both sides on grill and keep hot in foil. Slice meat thin across grain at a 30° angle. Spread bread (both halves) with the mustard butter. Overlap slices on one half of loaf, making double or triple layers. Sprinkle with pepper. Drizzle meat juice from slicing. Add top half of loaf. Cut on the bias into 8 sandwiches.

MEXICAN BEEF KABOBS

SAUCE:
½ C. chopped onion
1 T. olive oil
1 C. wine vinegar
½ tsp. salt
½ tsp. crushed oregano

½ tsp. cumin
½ tsp. cloves
½ tsp. cinnamon
½ tsp. pepper
1 clove garlic, minced

Cook onions in hot oil until tender. Add vinegar and seasonings and garlic. Cover and simmer 20 minutes. Cool.

Instant meat tenderizer

1½ lb. round steak, cut in 1½" cubes

Sprinkle tenderizer on meat according to label directions. Skewer meat. Brush with sauce. Broil over hot coals about 12 to 15 minutes for medium-rare, turning and basting often. Serves 4.

3

STEAK STRIPS

2 lb. round steak, cut 1½"
  thick
1 C. Russian salad dressing
2 T. lemon juice

15 medium-sized fresh
  mushrooms
15 cherry tomatoes
6-15" metal skewers

Cut steak into strips ¼" thick and place in plastic bag. Combine dressing, lemon juice and pour into bag with beef. Press air out and close securely. Marinate in refrigerator 4 to 6 hours or overnight. Pour off marinade and reserve. Thread beef on skewers, weaving back and forth. Alternate meat, mushrooms and tomatoes. Put skewers on grill and broil on moderate heat 3 minutes, brushing with marinade form time to time. Turn and grill 3 to 4 minutes. Serves 4 to 6.
NOTE: If steak is partially frozen, it is easier to slice and put on skewers.

HOBO BEEF DINNER

2 lb. round steak, cut
  ½" thick
3 T. flour
1 tsp. salt
¼ tsp. pepper
6 medium carrots, pared

¾ C. uncooked rice
6 bouillon cubes
3 C. water
6 clean 16 oz. cans
6-8" squares foil

Cut round steak in strips ½" wide and 2½ to 3" long. Combine flour, salt and pepper. Dredge meat in seasoned flour. Place beef strips in each can, dividing equally. Slice carrots into each can and add 2 tablespoons of rice and 1 bouillon cube to each. Pour ½ cup water into each can and cover with foil. Place cans on grill and cook on moderate heat until meat, carrots and rice are tender, 1½ to 2 hours. Serves 6.

BARBECUED MEAT STRIPS

Cut 1½ pounds partially frozen boneless sirloin steak into strips 6" long, 1½" wide and ⅛" thick. Combine and mix ⅔ cup soy sauce, ¼ cup brown sugar, ¼ cup dry sherry, 1 tablespoon oil, 1 teaspoon ginger and 1 small clove garlic (minced). Pour over steak; marinate 20 to 30 minutes. Thread meat on 6 to 8" skewers. Grill to desired doneness on small grill 4" above low burning charcoal, turning often. Yield 12 appetizers or 6 entree servings.

CHARCOAL-BROILED SIRLOIN STEAK

1 large sirloin steak
⅓ C. salad oil
⅓ C. red wine vinegar
2 cloves garlic, crushed

1 tsp. basil
½ tsp. salt
½ tsp. pepper

Trim excess fat from steak. Slash fat edge of steak at 1" intervals. Place steak in pan large enough so steak can lay flat. Combine remaining ingredients. Mix well and pour over steak. Cover. Chill 2 to 3 hours, turning several times. Start charcoal fire 30 to 40 minutes ahead of time. Rub hot grill with the beef fat you trimmed off. Broil 1½ to 2" steaks on rack 5 to 6" above coals or 1" steak 4½ to 5" above coals. Broil first side. Turn and brush with marinade. Broil second side. To test steak for doneness, cut a small slash in center of steak and examine color.

ISLAND TERIYAKI

½ C. soy sauce
¼ C. brown sugar
2 T. olive oil
1 tsp. ground ginger
¼ tsp. cracked pepper

2 cloves garlic, minced
1 ½ lb. top sirloin steak,
 1" thick and cut in strips
 ¼" wide
Canned water chestnuts

Combine soy sauce, brown sugar, oil, ginger, pepper and garlic. Mix well. Put sauce and meat in large enough bowl so sauce will cover meat. Stir and let stand 2 hours at room temperature. Lace meat accordion style on skewers. Place a water chestnut on end of each skewer. Broil over hot coals 10 to 12 minutes, medium-well. Less if rare or medium-rare is desired. Turn often and baste. Serves 4.

SWANK PORTERHOUSE

2-1¼ to 1½ lbs. Porterhouse steaks, cut 1½" thick or 2 lb. sirloin steak, cut 1½" thick
½ C. onions, chopped
1 large clove garlic, minced
3 T. butter or margarine
¼ C. dry red wine
2 T. soy sauce
1 C. sliced fresh mushrooms

Slash fat edge of steak about 1" apart, being careful not to cut into meat. Slicing from fat side, cut pockets in each side of meat, cutting almost to bone. In skillet, cook onion and garlic in 1 tablespoon of the butter. Season meat with salt and pepper and celery salt. Stuff pockets with onion mixture. Skewer closed. Combine wine and soy sauce and brush on steak. Broil over medium-high coals for 25 to 30 minutes (30 to 35 minutes for sirloin) for rare or until desired doneness, turning once. Brush occasionally with soy mixture. In small skillet, cook mushrooms in last 2 tablespoons butter until tender. Pour over steak. Slice across grain. Serves 4.

9

PEPPER STEAK

Select 4 to 5 pound sirloin steak, 1½" thick. Rub and press 2 teaspoons cracked or coarsely ground whole black pepper in each side, using the palms of the hand. Let stand at room temperature 1 to 1¼ hours. Broil on grill or hibachi over hot coals, 5" from coals, 9 to 11 minutes per side for medium doneness. Transfer to platter. Sprinkle with salt. When steak is about done, saute ½ cup sliced onions in 1 tablespoon butter and spoon over steak.

STEAK SUPREME

6 rib-eye steaks,
about 1½" thick
4 oz. bleu cheese

¼ C. butter or margarine
2 tsp. oregano leaves
2 tsp. seasoned pepper

Mix softened butter, bleu cheese, oregano and pepper together. Cook steaks on grill 5" from coals 6 minutes on each side. Turn steaks again and spread with cheese mixture. Cook 5 minutes longer for medium steaks. Serves 6.

STEAK SANDWICHES WITH APPLESAUCE

1 medium onion, sliced thin
¼ C. salad oil
1 C. canned applesauce
1 C. catsup
1 T. sugar
2 T. Worcestershire sauce

1 T. lemon juice
½ tsp. salt
½ tsp. crushed oregano
6 cube steaks
6 hamburger buns, split,
  toasted and buttered

In large skillet, cook onion in hot oil until tender, but not brown. Add applesauce, catsup and seasonings. Heat, stirring occasionally, until bubbling. Remove from heat. Add steaks, turning to coat and let stand 15 minutes. Lift out steaks and broil quickly over hot coals about 1 to 2 minutes per side, brushing with barbecue sauce after turning. Put steaks into buns and spoon extra sauce on meat. Serves 6.

GRILLED MINUTE OR CUBE STEAK

Marinate steaks 30 minutes before broiling. Drain well. Place on greased grill. Grill on medium-high 2 to 3" over heat until browned on both sides, turning steaks once. About 2 minutes on each side for medium-well done. MARINADE SAUCE: Combine 1 cup vinegar (wine, tarragon or cider), ½ cup each salad oil, sliced onions, 1 teaspoon salt, 2 cloves garlic (thinly sliced), 6 to 8 whole peppercorns and ¼ teaspoon each of leaf thyme and rosemary. Use leftover marinade for basting sauce. Yields 1¾ cups.

PIZZA STEAK SANDWICH

6 beef cube steaks
1-8 oz. can tomato sauce
¼ C. grated Parmesan
  cheese
1 tsp. instant minced onion
½ tsp. oregano
½ tsp. basil

½ tsp. garlic powder
6 large English muffins, split
12 small stuffed green
  olives, sliced
6 slices mozzarella cheese
Salt
Pepper
6-18" squares foil

Combine tomato sauce, Parmesan cheese, onion, oregano, basil and garlic powder. Cook slowly for 5 minutes. Broil steaks at medium over grill, 3 to 5 minutes on each side. Spread each of 6 muffin halves with 1 tablespoon of sauce and place steak on top. Spread steak with remaining sauce and top with olives. Cut cheese slices in half. Cross 2 strips and place on steak. Top with muffin top. Wrap each sandwich in foil. Place on grill over medium heat and cook about 5 minutes turning occasionally. Serves 6.

LONDON BROIL

1 beef flank steak,
  1½ to 1¾ lbs.
¼ C. salad oil
1 T. lemon juice

1 clove garlic, crushed
½ tsp. salt
¼ tsp. pepper

Combine salad oil, lemon juice, garlic, salt and pepper for marinade. Place steak in plastic bag or flat utility dish and pour marinade over it. Close bag securely or cover dish and refrigerate 4 to 6 hours. Pour off marinade and reserve. Place steak on grill and broil at moderate temperature 5 minutes. Turn. Brush with marinade and broil 5 minutes or to desired doneness (rare or medium). To carve, slice diagonally across grain in thin strips. Serves 4.

LONDON BROIL

Score a prime or choice grade flank steak (about 1½ pounds) with knife on top and bottom of steak, making the cuts about ¼" deep. Marinate steak or use a commercial meat tenderizer as package directs. Broil to rare stage on greased grill over hot coals, 4 to 7 minutes for each side. Don't broil flank steak too well done. The meat will become very tough. Brush meat with butter or your favorite marinade sauce several times during cooking. Season with salt and pepper. Yields 4 to 6 servings.

CHUCK WAGON STEAKS

2 beef blade steaks,
  cut ½ to ¾" thick
1 medium-sized onion,
  chopped
1 C. catsup
⅓ C. vinegar

2 T. brown sugar
2 tsp. salt
1 clove garlic, crushed
1 bay leaf
⅛ tsp. hot pepper sauce

Combine onion, catsup, vinegar, brown sugar, salt, garlic, bay leaf and hot sauce in saucepan and cook slowly for 10 minutes. Cool. Pour sauce over steaks in flat dish, turning to coat all sides. Marinate in refrigerator 4 hours or overnight. Pour off marinade and reserve. Place steaks on grill and broil at moderate temperature for 15 to 25 minutes, depending on thickness and degree of doneness desired. Turn and brush with sauce.

TINY CABBAGE ROLLS

Prepare your favorite hamburger mixture. Shape into rolls 1½" long and ½ to ¾" in diameter; chill. Saute meat rolls in butter until meat is cooked through, not brown. Brush meat rolls with Zippy Barbecue Sauce or catsup. Roll in wilted cabbage leaves. To wilt leaves, drop fresh cabbage leaves in boiling, salted water. Drain well. Wrap each meat roll in small cabbage leaf and thread on 6" skewer. Cut strips of foil ½" wider and longer than skewer. Arrange each on a piece of foil. Bring to serving temperature on hibachi or small grill 4" above medium heat. Brush with sauce and heat, turning once. Serve with barbecue sauce.

ZIPPY BARBECUE SAUCE: Combine ⅔ cup catsup, ¼ cup water or tomato juice, ⅓ cup each finely chopped onion and diced celery, 1½ tablespoons brown sugar and 2 tablespoons Worcestershire sauce. Simmer gently 12 to 15 minutes Yields 1¼ cups.

GOLDEN BEEF BALL KABOBS

3 lbs. ground beef
½ C. barbecue sauce
1 small onion, chopped
¼ C. flour
1 T. prepared mustard
1 T. salt
¼ tsp. pepper

8 oz. Cheddar cheese,
  cut in 24-¾" cubes
18 pieces dill pickles
6 metal 15" skewers
Barbecue sauce
12 cherry tomatoes

Thoroughly mix ground beef, barbecue sauce, onion, flour, mustard, salt and pepper. Divide mixture into 24 portions about ¼ cup each and form into balls, placing a cube of cheese in center of each. On each skewer, thread 4 meatballs alternately with 3 pieces of pickle. Place kabobs on greased grill top and broil at moderate temperature 6 minutes. Brush with barbecue sauce and broil 12 to 20 minutes, turning and brushing with barbecue sauce until done. Add 2 cherry tomatoes to end of each skewer last 3 minutes of cooking time. Serves 6.

TWIN BEEF BURGERS

2 lbs. ground beef
½ small head lettuce,
  shredded
2 small tomatoes, chopped
2 T. pickle relish
1 can (⅔ C.) evaporated
  milk
⅓ C. corn chips, crushed

⅓ C. catsup
2 tsp. salt
2 tsp. chili powder
2 T. corn chips, crushed
½ C. Cheddar cheese,
  shredded

Combine lettuce, tomatoes and pickle relish and chill. Lightly combine beef, milk, ⅓ cup corn chips, catsup, salt and chili powder. Shape into 2 patties, about 1" thick and 7" in diameter. Place on grill and broil at moderate temperature for 10 minutes. Turn with large spatula and broil 5 to 12 minutes longer. During last 2 to 3 minutes cooking, place shredded cheese on each patty and sprinkle with 1 tablespoon corn chips. Cut each beef burger in quarters and serve with lettuce-tomato mixture. Serves 8.   22

OUTDOOR BURGERS

1 lb. ground beef
¼ C. chopped onions
2 T. green pepper, chopped
 fine
3 T. catsup

1 T. prepared horseradish
1 tsp. salt
2 tsp. prepared mustard
Dash salt

Combine all ingredients. Mix lightly. Shape into 4 patties about ½" thick. Broil over hot coals about 5 minutes on each side. Serves 4.

LARGE BUNYANBURGERS

2 eggs	1½ tsp. salt
2 lbs. ground beef	½ tsp. garlic salt
2 T. Worcestershire sauce	Pepper

Beat eggs slightly. Add beef and seasonings. Mix lightly to blend. Use a 9" bake pan as a guide. Draw 3 circles on wax paper. Place a third of the meat mixture on each circle. Pat to fill circle.

FILLING: Leaving a 1" margin for sealing, spread half of patty with mustard. Top with chopped onion, cubed cheese, pickle relish or any other of your favorite burger toppings. fold meat over turnover fashion. Press around margins to seal. Brush top with melted butter to keep from sticking to grill. Place in basket broiler and brush other side with butter. Broil slowly to brown meat well and to completely heat filling. Makes 3 giant burgers.

COMPANY BURGERS

1-4 oz. can mushrooms
  (stems and pieces)
2 T. instant minced onion
1 T. dried chopped chives
1 tsp. curry powder
2 tsp. seasoned salt

½ tsp. lemon-pepper
  seasoning
½ tsp. salt
¼ tsp. monosodium
  glutamate
2 lbs. ground beef

Empty mushrooms, including juice, into a large bowl. Chop mushrooms into small pieces. Add the next 7 ingredients and let stand 5 minutes. Add meat and mix well. Let stand 10 minutes. Shape into 8 patties. Cook on grill 3" from medium coals, 3 to 4 minutes on each side. Serves 8.

GRILLED STUFFED CHEESEBURGERS

1½ lbs. ground beef
⅓ C. teriyaki sauce
¼ C. soft bread crumbs
1 egg

2 T. instant minced onion
¼ tsp. seasoned pepper
1 tsp. seasoned salt
½ C. shredded sharp
   Cheddar cheese

Combine the first 7 ingredients. Mix well. Let stand 10 minutes. Shape into 12 patties. Sprinkle cheese over 6 patties, leaving a ½" margin around edges. Top with remaining 6 patties. Pinch edges together to seal. Cook on grill 3" from coals, 3 to 4 minutes on each side or to desired doneness. Makes 6 servings.

STEAK BURGERS

2 lbs. ground lean beef
   chuck, round or sirloin tip
¼ C. finely chopped onion,
   optional

2 tsp. salt
⅛ tsp. pepper
Butter or margarine
Your favorite basting sauce

Combine meat, onions, salt and pepper. Mix. Shape into 6 or 8 patties ½ to ¾" thick. Grill medium-high 4 to 6 minutes for medium doneness.

ALOHA BURGERS

1-9 oz. can pineapple slices
1 lb. ground beef
1 tsp. salt

Dash of pepper
1 recipe Sauce

Drain pineapple. Reserve 2 tablespoons juice for sauce. Season meat with salt and pepper. Press tablespoon of meat into center of each pineapple slice, overlapping meat on pineapple around center on both sides of slice so meat won't fall out while cooking. Shape the rest of the hamburger into 4 patties, a little larger than pineapple slices. Broil burgers on grill over hot coals 12 to 15 minutes, turn once. Broil meat-filled pineapple slices, turning very carefully and brushing with sauce, until meat is done and pineapple glazed. To assemble, place each hamburger on a bun half. Top with pineapple slices. Top with a green olive.
SAUCE: Mix 2 tablespoons pineapple juice, ½ cup catsup, ¼ cup brown sugar, 2 teaspoons Worcestershire sauce and a few drops liquid smoke. Heat to boiling.

BARBECUED MEAT LOAVES

2 lbs. ground beef
2 eggs, beaten
2 C. soft bread crumbs
¼ C. onion, chopped fine
1 T. prepared horseradish

1½ tsp. salt
½ tsp. dry mustard
¼ C. milk
½ C. butter or margarine
½ C. catsup

Combine first 8 ingredients and mix well. Shape in 6 miniature loaves about 3x4". Place in wire broil basket. Heat butter with catsup just until butter melts. Brush on all sides of loaves. Cook over medium coals. Turn and brush all sides often with sauce. Cook 40 minutes or until done. Serves 6.

MINIATURE ALOHA MEAT LOAVES

2 lbs. ground beef
1 C. (8 oz.) tomato sauce
¾ C. crushed cracker
  crumbs
½ C. chopped onion
⅓ C. chopped green
  pepper
1 egg

1 T. soy sauce
1 tsp. salt
¼ tsp. ginger
8 pineapple rings
8 maraschino cherry halves
8 aluminum tart pans
8-6" squares foil

Thoroughly combine ground beef, tomato sauce, cracker crumbs, onions, green pepper, egg, soy sauce, salt and ginger. Place pineapple ring on bottom of tart pan and 1 cherry half (cut side up) in each ring. Divide beef in eighths and place one portion in each pan. Cover tightly with aluminum foil. Place on grill over low to moderate heat for 40 to 60 minutes or until done. Uncover. Pour off drippings and invert pans on hot dishes. Serves 8. These can be made ahead and frozen.

BEEF WITH DEVILED HAM

3 lbs. beef, round
1 clove garlic, minced
2 T. chopped parsley
2 T. thyme
2 T. grated lemon rind
1½ tsp. salt

½ tsp. pepper
1-3 oz. can grated
  Parmesan cheese
1 C. dry sherry wine
1-4½ oz. can deviled ham

Pound the beef round with dull edge of a heavy knife. Then cut 2 or 3" squares. Place in shallow dish. Combine garlic, parsley, thyme, lemon rind, salt, pepper, cheese and wine. Pour over beef. Cover and marinate in refrigerator overnight. Cut six 7" squares of foil. Spread the center of each with deviled ham. Place beef on top and seal securely. Start grill. Let coals become gray ash before cooking meat, place packets of meat on grill and cook 10 to 12 minutes on each side. Serves 6.

KOREAN MEAT PATTIES

1 lb. ground beef
1 egg
¼ C. fine dry bread crumbs
2 T. chopped green onion

1 T. soy sauce
½ tsp. sugar
½ tsp. salt
6 to 8 drops hot pepper
   sauce

Combine and mix all ingredients together and shape into 1½" patties. Barbecue on a small grill 3" from medium heat, 5 to 7 minutes to desired doneness, turning once. Serve on picks with Sashimi Sauce. Yields 3 dozen.

SASHIMI SAUCE: Combine and mix ½ cup soy sauce, 1 tablespoon prepared horseradish, 1 teaspoon sugar and ½ teaspoon dry mustard. Yields ½ cup.

BURGUNDY BEEFBURGERS

2 lbs. ground chuck
1 C. soft bread crumbs
1 egg
¼ C. Burgundy wine
2 T. green onions, sliced

1 tsp. salt
Dash pepper
Kitchen Bouquet
Burgundy Sauce

Lightly stir ground chuck, crumbs, egg, Burgundy wine, onions, salt and pepper with fork until well mixed. Shape in 8 patties, about ½" thick. Brush patties on both sides with Kitchen Bouquet. Grill over hot coals for 5 minutes. Turn and broil 3 to 4 more minutes or until done. Brush often with Burgundy Sauce. Serves 8.

BURGUNDY SAUCE: Cook 2 tablespoons sliced green onions in ½ cup butter until tender, but not brown. Stir in ¼ cup Burgundy wine.

GRILL-TOP POT-ROAST WITH GRAVY

3 to 4 lb. beef blade pot roast
1 C. catsup
¼ C. flour
1 T. lemon juice

2 tsp. salt
¼ tsp. pepper
2 medium onions, sliced
Enough heavy-duty foil
  (double thickness) to
  wrap roast

Arrange half onions on foil. Combine catsup, flour, lemon juice, salt and pepper. Spread half mixture over onion slices. Place roast on onion slices. Spread beef with remaining catsup mixture and put remaining onions on roast. Fold edges of foil around roast, leaving air space. Place on grill and cook on low temperature until tender, 2 to 3 hours, turning carefully. Open foil and remove roast to hot platter. Remove gravy from foil using rubber spatula and serve with pot roast.

BARBECUED SIRLOIN TIP

4 to 6 lb. beef sirloin tip   Barbecue sauce
    roast, tied

Insert rotisserie rod lengthwise through center of roast. Balance roast and tighten spit forks to hold meat secure. Insert meat thermometer at a slight angle. Place on rotisserie and roast at moderate temperature until thermometer registers 130°. Continue roasting, brushing frequently with sauce, to desired doneness, 140 to 160°. Allow roast to stand 10 to 15 minutes before carving.

KETTLE POT ROAST

Select a 6 to 9 pound beef pot roast, 3 to 4" thick. Rub with olive oil, salt and pepper. Place on grill top of coals and sear roast on both sides. Baste with sauce of sour cream with a dash of garlic powder and prepared horseradish to suit your taste. Cover barbecue kettle with lid (or lower hood). Cook slowly about 15 minutes per pound for medium rare. Every 15 minutes baste with sour cream sauce.

RUMP ROAST

1-3 lb. rolled rump roast
½ C. soy sauce
¼ C. salad oil

½ tsp. lemon-pepper
  seasoning
½ tsp. seasoned salt
¼ C. Pinot Noir wine

Place roast in bowl. Combine remaining ingredients. Pour over roast. Marinate 6 to 24 hours in the refrigerator, turning several times. Cook on spit over hot coals about 2 hours, basting often with remaining marinade. Serves 4 to 5.

ROLLED RIB ROAST

1 rolled rib roast (5 to 6 lbs.)
¼ C. butter or margarine,
softened
1 T. instant minced onion

1 tsp. marjoram leaves
1 tsp. dill seed
½ tsp. dry mustard
¼ tsp. garlic powder

Insert a knife into the roast, the full length of the blade at 2" intervals. Blend the butter, onion, marjoram, dill seed, dry mustard and garlic powder together. Put some of the seasoned butter in each slit, using all the butter mixture. Rub salt and pepper on outside of roast. Place spit on rotisserie 5 to 6" from coals. Cook about 1½ hours or to desired doneness. Serves 8 to 10.

RIB-EYE ON THE SPIT

5 to 6 lb. eye of rib roast
½ C. salad oil
½ C. soy sauce
½ C. bourbon whiskey
2 small onions, sliced thin
2 cloves garlic, chopped

2 T. fresh ginger, chopped
   (or 3 T. preserved ginger)
1 tsp. fresh ground pepper
1 tsp. dry mustard
¼ C. wine vinegar

Combine all marinade ingredients, pour over roast and let stand in this mixture for 1 hour, turning often. Prepare charcoal 30 minutes ahead of time. Soak 2 handfuls of hickory chips in water for 30 minutes. Bank coals at back of firebox. Make a drip pan from foil wider and longer than the roast. Place in front of coals to catch drippings. Now, put hickory chips on coals. Place roast on motor driven spit over coals. Cook roast, hood down, for 1 to 1½ hours, depending on desired doneness. Serves 6 to 8.

CORNED BEEF ROAST

3 to 4 lb. corned beef
  brisket
½ C. brown sugar

½ tsp. cloves
½ tsp. dry mustard
½ tsp. ginger

Simmer corned beef as directed on package label. Drain and pat dry. Combine next 4 ingredients together and rub roast with mixture. Fasten securely in spit basket. Cook over low to medium low coals 4 to 5" from heat 1 to 1¼ hours. Serves 8.

ZESTY BEEF BRISKET

3 to 5 lb. beef brisket
Water to cover
2 tsp. salt
¼ tsp. pepper
1 medium onion, sliced

½ C. catsup
2 T. brown sugar
1 T. Worcestershire sauce
1 tsp. instant coffee, freeze-
dried or powdered

Cover beef brisket with water and add salt, pepper and onion. Cover and simmer slowly 3 hours or until tender. Combine catsup, brown sugar, Worcestershire sauce and instant coffee. Remove meat from liquid. Brush both sides with sauce and place on grill. Cook at moderate temperature for 15 to 20 minutes, turning and brushing with sauce. Carve diagonally into thin slices.

GOURMET BEEF TENDERLOIN

4 to 6 lb. beef tenderloin
4 oz. bleu cheese

1 T. Worcestershire sauce
1 T. chopped chives

Place beef on grill 3 to 5" from coals and cook at moderate temperature for 30 to 60 minutes, depending on size of tenderloin and desired doneness. Blend bleu cheese with Worcestershire sauce and stir in chives. Spread cheese mixture on top of meat 5 to 10 minutes before end of cooking time.

ISLAND STEAK

1 butt beef tenderloin,
about 2½ to 3 lbs.
3 T. butter
1 small onion, diced

12 mushrooms, sliced
½ C. brandy
½ tsp. tarragon

Saute onions in butter until soft and brown, then add mushrooms, brandy and tarragon. Simmer until mixture is thick. Make an incision in the beef tenderloin, cutting lengthwise and almost all the way through. Stuff with mixture, then close gap with foil and tie meat in 3 or 4 places. Put on spit and charcoal broil about 40 to 45 minutes for rare. Baste often with more butter and 1 tablespoon brandy.

TENDERLOIN STRIPS

2 lb. beef tenderloin
½ C. vegetable oil
1 large Bermuda onion,
cut into wedges
2 green peppers, cut
in strips

1 small can (2 oz.) pimentos,
drained and chopped
2 cloves garlic
Juice of 1 lemon
1 tsp. salt
½ tsp. pepper
Quilted broiler foil

Make a pan by cutting a 14" square of quilted broiler foil, folding a double 1½" edge on all four sides, making diagonal folds at corners and bringing these corners back against the sides. Let the coals burn down until coals are covered with gray ashes. Cut beef into strips 2" long and ½" square. Set aside. In foil pan, cook onions and peppers in oil until slightly brown and tender. Add pimentos and meat. Cook until browned. Mash garlic. Combine juice with lemon juice and add to meat mixture. Season with salt and pepper and cook 3 to 4 minutes longer. 44

CAMP-OUT BEEF SOUP

2 lb. boneless beef,
  cut in 1" cubes
2-11½ oz. cans condensed
  bean soup
4½ C. water
1 medium onion, chopped
2 tsp. salt

1 tsp. basil
¼ tsp. pepper
1-5½ oz. pkg. dehydrated
  hash brown potatoes with
  onion
2-16 oz. cans tomatoes
2 medium carrots, sliced thin

Combine bean soup and water in large Dutch oven or pot, suitable for grill or hanging over coals on ground. Add beef cubes, onion, salt; basil and pepper and bring to boil. Cook 1½ hours or until meat is done. Add potatoes, tomatoes and carrots. Cover and cook about 30 to 40 minutes more. Serves 8 to 10.

PATIO DINNER

½ C. finely chopped onion
1 clove garlic, minced
3 T. olive oil
1 T. flour
1-10 oz. can tomato puree
½ C. water
1 to 2 T. chili powder
1 tsp. salt
¼ tsp. oregano
¼ tsp. cumin
¼ C. onion, chopped

1 lb. boneless lean beef chuck or stew meat, cut in 1" cubes
1-12 oz. can whole kernel corn
1-10 oz. pkg. frozen lima beans
1 onion, sliced, separated in rings
1 C. sharp cheese, shredded
1-6 oz. pkg. corn chips

Cook ½ cup onion and garlic in 3 tablespoons olive oil until tender. Stir in flour. Add tomatoes, water and seasonings. Simmer 10 minutes in large kettle over medium-high grill. Tear off four 12" lengths of 18" wide foil. On each place G of the meat. Top with vegetables. Drizzle each serving with ½ cup sauce. Bring edges of foil up and leaving room for expansion of steam, seal well with double foil. Place on grill and cook over coals until meat is tender, about 1½ hours, turning once. When serving, cut a crisscross in top of foil. Sprinkle each dinner with cheese, chopped onion and corn chips. Makes 4 servings.

ORIENTAL-STYLE SHORT RIBS

4 lbs. beef short ribs
⅓ C. soy sauce
⅓ C. cooking oil
⅓ C. sherry or pineapple
  juice

⅓ C. lemon juice
3 T. brown sugar
½ tsp. ginger

Mix all ingredients except meat for marinade. Trim excess fat from short ribs. Arrange in a shallow baking dish. Pour marinade over meat. Cover and refrigerate 2 to 3 hours. Drain ribs. Arrange bone side down on grill 5 to 6" over low to medium heat (325 to 350°). Cover grill and cook 1 to 1¼ hours, basting frequently. Serves 4.

BARBECUED SHORT RIBS

5 lbs. lean short ribs,
  3 to 4" long
⅔ C. teriyaki sauce

¼ C. orange marmalade
1 tsp. garlic salt
½ tsp. lemon-pepper
  seasoning

Place short ribs in large bowl. Combine remaining ingredients. Pour over ribs. Cover and refrigerate 8 to 10 hours, turn occasionally. Remove from marinade and drain. Cook slowly on grill 7 to 8" from coals, 1½ to 2 hours or until meat begins to leave bone. Turn often. Brush with marinade during last 20 minutes of cooking. Serves 4 to 6.

CHINESE APPETIZER RIBS

Place 3 pounds baby spareribs (or regular size ribs, cut 3" wide) in plastic bag in long flat pan. Add Chinese Marinade to bag and tie with string. Put in refrigerator 2 to 4 hours, turning bag over 2 or 3 times. Drain ribs well. Save marinade. Arrange ribs on hibachi or small grill, 5 to 7" from medium heat. Baste with marinade until ribs are tender, 1 to 1¼ hours.

CHINESE MARINADE: Combine and mix ⅓ cup each soy sauce, cooking oil, sherry or pineapple juice and lemon juice, 3 tablespoons brown sugar and ½ teaspoon ginger. Use leftover marinade for basting sauce. Yields 1⅓ cups.

GRILLED SPARERIBS

2 envs. herb or French salad
   dressing mix
½ C. dark corn syrup

¼ C. vinegar
3 T. brown sugar
4 lbs. lean spareribs

Combine salad dressing mix, corn syrup, vinegar and brown sugar. Stir well and set aside. Place ribs bone side down on grill over slow coals. Broil about 20 minutes. Turn meaty side down and broil until browned. Turn meat side up again and broil 20 more minutes. Brush with basting sauce and broil 20 to 30 minutes or until done. Serves 4.

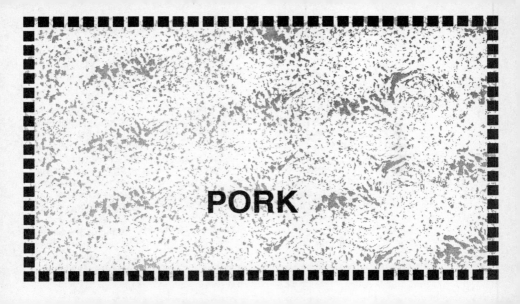

PORK

APPLE-RAISIN PORK CHOPS

6 pork rib chops, 1" thick
¼ C. milk
1 C. soft bread crumbs
⅛ tsp. salt
¼ tsp. sage

1 C. finely chopped apples
½ C. raisins
1 T. melted butter
1 tsp. salt
⅛ tsp. pepper

Make a pocket in each chop by cutting into the chop along the bone. Pour milk over crumbs. Stir in salt, apples, raisins and melted butter. Stuff each chop with ¼ cup apple mixture. Grill over medium coals about 1 hour or until well done. Serves 6.

FARMLAND PORK CHOPS

Soak the chops in milk to cover, which has been seasoned with salt and pepper to taste and 2 cloves garlic, chopped fine. Let chops set 6 to 8 hours refrigerated. Remove slowly 4 to 6" over coals about 1 hour. Use the milk marinade to make cream gravy.

GRILLED PORK CHOPS
(FRESH OR SMOKED)

Select fresh chops about 1" thick and arrange on well-greased hibachi or grill or hinged broiler. Place 4 to 6" from low to medium heat. Brown chops on first side 15 to 18 minutes. Turn chops. Barbecue until well browned. Brush meat often during cooking with oil, butter or basting sauce.

HERBED PORK CHOPS

Cover pork chops with tomato juice which has been well seasoned with salt and coarsely ground black pepper and plenty of crushed basil leaves. Let chops marinate for 6 hours. Remove, making certain that the basil clings to the chops. Broil slowly 4 to 6" over coals until done, about 1 hour.

BEER BATTER PORK CHOPS

8 medium-sized loin pork
 chops
¼ lb. butter
2 oranges or tangerines

1 C. flour
1 tsp. salt
¼ tsp. pepper
1 can beer

Start grill and let fire burn until gray ashes cover coals. Use a foil pan about 14x10". Put butter in pan and melt on grill 2" above coals. Squeeze juice from oranges into a 1½-quart bowl. Add flour, seasonings and beer. Mix well. Dip chops in batter and brown on both sides in the melted butter. Raise grill to 5 or 6" above coals. Place chops on grill and cook about 15 minutes on each side. Serves 4 to 8.

BEST BARBECUED RIBS

1 C. catsup
1 T. Worcestershire sauce
2 or 3 dashes bottled hot
  pepper sauce
¼ C. vinegar

1 T. sugar
1 tsp. salt
1 tsp. celery seed
4 lbs. pork spareribs
1 lemon, thinly sliced
1 large onion, thinly sliced

SAUCE: Combine catsup, Worcestershire sauce, hot pepper sauce, ½ cup water, vinegar, sugar, salt and celery seed. Simmer 20 minutes, stirring occasionally. Salt ribs and place on rack over slow coals. Put barbecue hood down. Cook 1 hour. Brush with sauce. Attach lemon and onion slices on ribs with toothpicks. Continue cooking, without turning, 30 to 40 minutes or until done. Serves 4.

PEANUT BUTTERED PORK LOIN

2 boned pork loins   ½ C. orange juice
  (5 to 6 lbs. total)   ¼ C. creamy peanut butter

Tie pork loins together at 1½" intervals with fat sides out. Balance roast on spit and secure with holding forks. Insert meat thermometer. Season with salt and pepper. Arrange medium coals. Place a foil drip pan under roast. Attach spit. Turn on motor and lower hood. Roast to 170°, about 3 hours. Combine orange juice and peanut butter. When meat is done, brush sauce on roast and continue cooking and basting 15 to 20 minutes. Serves 15.

PORK CUBES

Brown 1½ pounds boneless lean pork cubes in 1 tablespoon hot shortening, until tender. Pour Kabob Marinade over meat. Refrigerate until ready to cook. Pour mixture into heavy shallow covered pan. Heat on hibachi or small grill 4 to 5" above low burning charcoal. Serves 10 to 12 appetizers. Serve with Mustard Honey Sauce.

KABOB MARINADE: Combine ⅓ cup each soy sauce and lemon juice, ¼ cup each honey and grenadine or water and 1 teaspoon salt. Use leftover marinade for basting. Yields 1 cup.

MUSTARD HONEY SAUCE: Combine and mix ½ cup honey, ¾ cup ginger ale, 1 tablespoon cornstarch, ¼ cup prepared mustard and ½ teaspoon prepared horseradish. Cook over low heat until sauce is clear and thick. Yields 1½ cups sauce.

HAM MANDARIN

1 slice tenderized ham,
  center cut (1" thick)
1-11 oz. can mandarin
  oranges
½ C. port wine
½ C. plum jam

3 T. wine vinegar
½ tsp. Kitchen Bouquet
3 T. grated orange rind
2 T. cornstarch
½ tsp. allspice
½ tsp. dry mustard

Drain oranges. Combine juice, port wine, plum jam, vinegar, Kitchen Bouquet, grated rind, cornstarch, allspice and dry mustard in blender. Blend and pour in saucepan. Simmer until mixture reduces to half the original amount. Chill. Trim all fat and rind from ham. Place on a sheet of foil 3 times the size of the ham. Spread sauce over ham and garnish with orange segments. Fold the ends of foil over each other, sealing tightly. Place top side down on the grill over coals that have been burned down to gray ashes. Cook 10 minutes. Turn and cook 20 minutes more.

GRILL-GLAZED HAM SLICES

Score edges of fully-cooked ham slices (1" thick). Grill over slow coals 10 to 15 minutes on each side. A few minutes before done, brush with glaze.

GLAZE: Drain ½ cup syrup from spiced crab apples. Combine syrup and 1 cup brown sugar in saucepan. Heat until sugar dissolves, stirring constantly. Warm apples in remaining syrup and serve with ham slices. Makes 4 servings.

ORANGE GLAZED HAM

¼ C. frozen orange juice
  concentrate
¼ C. cooking sherry
1 tsp. dry mustard

¼ tsp. herbs
1-1" slice cooked ham,
  about 1½ lbs.
4 to 6 canned pineapple
  slices

Combine first 4 ingredients for sauce. Brush on ham. Grill over hot coals 6 to 8 minutes on each side or until browned, basting often. The last few minutes grill pineapple slices 2 to 3 minutes on each side until browned, basting often with sauce. Makes 4 to 6 servings. Serve pineapple slices on ham slices.

HAM

Use round, boneless, fully-cooked ham. Slit casing lengthwise and remove. Score ham. Tie with cord if necessary. Center lengthwise on spit; adjust on rotisserie. Let rotate over medium coals until hot through, about 10 minutes per pound. The last 20 minutes, brush with Glaze.

GLAZE: Drain 1-8½ ounce can crushed pineapple, reserving 2 tablespoons syrup. Mix reserved juice, pineapple, 1 cup brown sugar, 2 tablespoons lemon juice and 2 tablespoons prepared mustard.

SPICY FRANKS

1 C. apricot preserves
½-8 oz. can tomato sauce
⅓ C. vinegar
¼ C. dry white wine
2 T. soy sauce

2 T. honey
1 T. cooking oil
1 tsp. salt
¼ tsp. ground ginger
2 lbs. frankfurters

Combine all ingredients except franks. Score franks on the bias. Broil over hot coals, turning and basting often with sauce. Heat remaining sauce to pass when serving. Makes 6 to 10 servings.

HOT DOG BURGERS

1 egg, beaten
1 lb. ground beef
1 T. Worcestershire sauce
¾ tsp. salt

¾ tsp. seasoned salt
6 frankfurters
6 coney buns, split, toasted,
  buttered

Combine first 5 ingredients, mixing well. Wrap each frank with beef mixture. Spread outside with soft butter. Grill over hot coals about 13 minutes, turning often to cook all sides. Serve in hot buns with hot dog relish, prepared mustard and catsup. Serves 6.

SMOKING GOOD FRANKFURTERS

2 C. finely chopped onions
¼ C. salad oil
1-14 oz. bottle (1¼ C.)
  catsup
½ C. water
¼ C. brown sugar
1 T. vinegar

2 T. Worcestershire sauce
½ tsp. dry mustard
1 tsp. salt
1 tsp. liquid smoke
1½ doz. frankfurters

Cook onions in hot salad oil until almost tender. Add remaining ingredients except franks and simmer 15 minutes. (This can be done on the grill or ahead of time.) Score the franks in corkscrew fashion, cutting round and round. Roast on grill top or in wire broiler over hot coals. Drop into sauce to keep hot until serving time or put them in buns and spoon on sauce. Serves 9.

CIRCLE PUPS

1-1 lb. can (2 C.) sauerkraut
1 T. flour
1 tsp. sage

1 lb. (8 to 10) franks
8 to 10 slices rye bread,
 buttered
Prepared mustard

Drain kraut, reserving ½ cup juice. Mix flour, sage and juice. Stir into the drained kraut. Heat and stir until mixture thickens. At ½" intervals, cut slits across franks, going almost but not quite through. Broil franks over hot coals until hot through. They will curl as they cook. Place franks on bread. Fill center with hot kraut. Top with mustard.

FRANK OR SAUSAGE SANDWICH
(PIZZA STYLE)

Split 8 long (5 to 6") hard rolls in half. Spread cut side with onion butter. Combine and mix 2 cups shredded mozzarella cheese, ½ cup shredded Parmesan cheese and 2 teaspoons oregano. Sprinkle an equal amount of cheese mixture over bottom of each roll. Cover with other half of roll. Wrap in double thickness of foil. Place to one end of grill 4 to 6" from heat while franks, wieners, smoked sausage links or knockwurst heat and brown. To serve, unwrap roll. Open bun and carefully place hot sausage links on cheese. Serves 8.

ONION BUTTER: Stir 1 envelope (1⅜ ounces) dry onion soup mix and 1 teaspoon finely chopped parsley into 1 cup soft butter or margarine. Stir until smooth.

BACON APPETIZERS

Wrap any of the following with a slice of bacon. Secure with wooden pick or thread 2 or 3 varieties on 4 or 5" skewers. To cook, place skewers on small grill 4 to 5" above low burning coals. Heat and barbecue until food is hot and bacon is crisp and brown. Baste often with butter or your favorite basting sauce.

Cooked shrimp
Cooked lobster tails,
* sliced (1")*
Raw scallops
Sauteed chicken livers

Marinated cooked chicken or
* turkey cubes*
Wiener chunks
Vienna sausages
Pineapple chunks
Canned mushrooms

BARBECUED BOLOGNA

1-3 or 4 lb. big bologna,
  unsliced
1 C. catsup
⅓ C. butter or margarine,
  melted

1½ T. Worcestershire sauce
1½ T. brown prepared
  mustard
1½ tsp. onion salt

Score bologna with diagonal lines about ¼" deep. Anchor on spit. Attach to grill. (Place foil drip pan below, if your barbecue does not have a built in drip catcher.) Cook on rotisserie with hood down over medium coals for 1¼ hours or until completely heated through, nice and brown. Meanwhile, combine remaining ingredients for the basting sauce. Brush on bologna frequently the last 15 minutes of cooking. Slice about ¼" thick and serve between toasted buns with remaining sauce heated and spooned over.

LUNCH KABOBS

Thread 1½" squares of canned luncheon meat on skewers with quartered orange wedges (peel on) and canned sweet potatoes. Broil over slow coals, turning often and brush with glaze.

GLAZE: Combine ½ cup brown sugar, ½ cup orange juice, ¼ cup vinegar and 1 tablespoon prepared mustard. Simmer 10 minutes, uncovered.

PIGS IN BACON

Cut lengthwise slit in frankfurters, not quite through. Spoon mustard or catsup in slits. Fill slits with strips of cheese. Or, fill slits with drained sauerkraut seasoned with caraway seed. Wrap each frank with bacon strip, anchoring ends with toothpicks. Broil over hot coals, turning once until bacon is crisp. Serve in hot buttered buns.

BARBECUED PIGLET

Whole piglet, 25 to 35 lbs.
6 T. salt
1 tsp. pepper
1 tsp. garlic salt
1 lb. green onions,
  tops included
2 lbs. apples
Large red apple for garnish

BASTING SAUCE:
⅔ C. wine vinegar
⅔ C. lemon juice
⅔ C. salad oil
3 garlic cloves, chopped
1 tsp. soy sauce
1 tsp. salt
¼ tsp. freshly ground pepper

Use whole clean piglet. Combine salt, pepper and garlic salt and rub ⅔ of mixture into the cavity of the piglet, saving the other ⅓ for the outside. Stuff the cavity with the green onions and apples, which have been halved and cored, but unpeeled. Using metal skewers, truss the cavity with heavy cord or wire. Place pig on spit 6 foot long, fastening securely to spit with wire or cord wound crisscross fashion around body of piglet. Start spit. Make sure that spit turns in front of, not over, coals so the drippings will not drop in fire. Use a drop pan to catch the fats while roasting. Baste occasionally with sauce. Test piglet after 3 hours of cooking. It may take 5 hours to cook well done. To serve, place a red apple in piglet's mouth.

STUFFED LEG OF LAMB

1 lemon
2 oranges
1-6 or 7 lb. leg of lamb,
  boned
2 cloves garlic, crushed
Salt and coarse ground
  pepper

1 C. water
¼ C. butter or margarine
1 tsp. whole thyme
1-8 oz. pkg. (3½ C.) herb-
  seasoned stuffing

Cut peeling from lemon and oranges into paper thin strips. Section both oranges. Rub inside surface of meat with crushed garlic and sprinkle with salt and pepper. Scatter peeling over. Bring water, butter and thyme to boiling. When butter has melted, drizzle over stuffing, tossing to mix. Spoon about 2 cups stuffing on half of meat (the short way) and press double row or orange sections down center. Fold other half of meat over stuffing to make a square roast. Skewer the three open sides. Lace shut. Tie tightly with a string at 1½" intervals. Center roast on spit and continue on rotisserie for 2 to 2½ hours. Makes 10 to 12 servings. About 45 minutes before roast is done, wrap remaining stuffing in foil. Heat on grill, turning occasionally.

GRILLED LAMB CHOPS OR STEAKS

Trim excess fat from meat and marinate. Drain. Arrange ¾ to 1" apart on well-greased grill 3" above heat and sear quickly on both sides, turning once. Lower heat or raise grill and continue barbecuing meat 4" from medium heat until tender. Allow 10 to 15 minutes per side for a 1" chop or steak. Brush with marinade while cooking.

MINT MARINADE:
1-8 oz. jar mint jelly   *½ C. light corn syrup*
½ tsp. mint extract

Heat mint jelly and corn syrup slowly until jelly melts. Stir in ½ teaspoon mint extract. Baste meat 3 or 4 times during cooking.

SWEET 'N SOUR SAUCE MARINADE (For Grilled Lamb Chops or Steaks): Combine and mix ¾ cup orange juice, ½ cup sweet sherry, ¼ cup each of vinegar or lemon juice and minced parsley, 3 tablespoons honey or sugar, 1 teaspoon each of basil and rosemary and ½ teaspoon salt.

GRILL-ROASTED LAMB

Have a 6-pound leg of lamb boned and flattened. Marinate 2 hours at room temperature in a mixture of 1 cup salad oil, ¼ cup wine vinegar, 1 tablespoon salt, ¼ teaspoon each garlic salt and garlic powder. Mix 2 cups chopped onions, 2½ cups chili sauce, ½ cup lemon juice, ⅓ cup salad oil, 2 tablespoons vinegar, 2 teaspoons hot pepper sauce, 1 teaspoon minced canned green chilies, 1 tablespoon brown sugar, 1 teaspoon each salt and dry mustard, 1 bay leaf, crushed. Simmer 20 minutes. Roast meat on grill over medium coals 2 hours. Turn every 15 minutes and baste with chili sauce mixture. Slice cross-grain. Serves 8 to 10.

ARMENIAN SHISH KABOBS

½ C. cooking oil
¼ C. lemon juice
1 tsp. dried marjoram,
   crushed
1 tsp. dried thyme, crushed
½ tsp. pepper
1 clove garlic, minced

½ C. chopped onions
¼ C. snipped parsley
2 lbs. boneless lamb,
   cut in 1½" cubes
Sweet red and green
   peppers, quartered
Onions wedges, precooked

Combine oil, lemon juice, 1 teaspoon salt, marjoram, thyme, pepper, garlic, onion and parsley. Add meat and stir to coat. Let set overnight or several hours in refrigerator, turning meat occasionally. Fill skewers with meat cubes, chunks of green and red peppers and onion wedges. Broil over hot coals, 10 to 12 minutes, turning and brushing often with marinade. Serve 6.

LAMB RIBS

3 to 4 lbs. lamb ribs, cut
  in serving pieces
Salt and pepper
¾ C. catsup
¾ C. water
½ C. chopped onion
2 T. brown sugar

3 T. lemon juice
3 T. Worcestershire sauce
2 T. vinegar
1½ tsp. monosodium
  glutamate
¾ tsp. salt
Dash bottled hot pepper
  sauce

Brown ribs on grill over hot coals with hickory added, turning often. This takes about 15 to 20 minutes. Season with salt and pepper. Meanwhile, combine remaining ingredients. Transfer meat to skillet and pour sauce over. Cover. Simmer over low to medium heat on grill about 1 hour. Remove excess fat. Serves 4 to 5.

VEAL CHOPS

Loin chops may be grilled if the process is a slow one, with low heat and basting. Use chops 1½ to 2" thick. Butter or oil chops well or roll a strip of bacon around each one and secure with a small skewer. Grill slowly over low temperature coals and turn often. It takes 25 to 30 minutes for well done chops. Meat should be white and juicy. Salt and pepper when they are removed from the fire.

FISH & POULTRY

BARBECUED SHRIMP

Combine and mix 3 pounds large shrimp, peeled and deveined and Wine Marinade in bowl. Cover and refrigerate 2 to 4 hours, stirring often. Thread shrimp on skewer. Cook by holding over medium or medium-high grill, 4 to 6" from coals until shrimp are pink and cooked. Serves 3 to 4.

WINE MARINADE: Combine 1 cup each pineapple juice, white wine, 1/3 cup lemon juice, 1 teaspoon grated lemon rind, 1 tablespoon Worcestershire sauce, 1 teaspoon thyme, 1/2 teaspoon each salt and rosemary and 1/4 teaspoon pepper. Use for basting. Yields 2 1/2 cups.

BARBECUED SHRIMP WITH LEMON

3 large cloves garlic, sliced
4 T. butter or margarine

12 oz. cleaned raw shrimp
 (1½ lbs. in shell)
½ lemon, sliced paper thin
Snipped parsley

Cook garlic in butter 2 or 3 minutes. Line a shallow pan with foil. Arrange shrimp in a layer over bottom. Sprinkle with salt and pepper. Place lemon slices over shrimp. Drizzle with garlic butter. Sprinkle with parsley. Cover over hot coals 6 to 8 minutes. Turn often. Serves 3.

SEAFOOD KABOBS

¼ C. soy sauce
¼ C. salad oil
¼ C. lemon juice
¼ C. minced parsley
½ tsp. salt

Dash pepper
Fresh or frozen shrimp
Fresh or frozen scallops
Large stuffed green olives
Lemon wedges

Combine first 6 ingredients for the basting sauce. Peel and devein shrimp, leaving last section of shell and tail intact. Add shrimp and scallops to sauce and let stand 1 hour at room temperature, stirring occasionally. On skewers, alternate shrimp, scallops, olives and lemon wedges. Broil over hot coals, turning and basting frequently. Don't overcook.

BARBECUED LOBSTER TAIL

Remove swimmerettes and sharp edges from 6 (8 ounces) fresh or defrosted frozen spiny or rock lobster tails. Cut off thin undershell membrane and any boney material with kitchen scissors. Wash and dry. Bend tail backwards to crack shell. Place lobster, shell side up, on oiled grill. Brush meat side with Lemony Butter. Close lid and cook on medium coals, 5 to 7" from heat and cook 3 to 5 minutes or until browned. Turn. Brush meat with butter and cook until meat is firm and opaque, 12 to 15 minutes. Allow one 8 ounce lobster tail per person.

LEMONY BUTTER AND BASTING SAUCE: Blend 3 tablespoons lemon juice, 2 tablespoons minced parsley and $\frac{1}{2}$ teaspoon grated lemon rind into 1 cup butter or margarine until spreadable. Yields 1$\frac{1}{4}$ cups.

OYSTERS ON PICKS

Sprinkle canned or fresh oysters with minced parsley and salt as desired. Wrap each oyster in a half slice of bacon. Secure with wooden picks. Place on small grill 4 to 5" from low heat until oysters have cooked and bacon is crisp, 4 to 6 minutes. Turn carefully once or twice during cooking. Baste with barbecue sauce if desired.

BARBECUED TROUT

6 medium dressed trout
Salt
⅓ C. sherry
⅓ C. melted butter
2 T. lemon juice
6 slices bacon

SAUCE:
2 tsp. sesame seeds
¼ C. butter
1 T. sherry
1 T. lemon juice

Sprinkle trout cavity with salt. Combine sherry, butter and lemon juice and pour over trout to marinate for 1 hour, turning once after 30 minutes. Remove trout and wrap each with strip of bacon. Cook trout over medium-hot coals until bacon is crisp, basting 3 or 4 times with remaining marinade. Turn once only. While trout is cooking, brown sesame seeds in butter. Add sherry and lemon juice. Serve hot over trout. Serves 6.

FRIED TROUT ALMONDINE

2 or more small cleaned
   trout
Salt, pepper, dried
   tarragon to taste
½ C. milk

½ C. flour
¼ lb. butter
¼ C. almonds, shredded
1 T. chopped parsley
Juice of 1 lemon

Wipe trout dry and dust with salt, pepper and a pinch of tarragon. Dip in milk then in flour. Saute fish over medium-hot coals in butter until brown. Remove from skillet onto platter (keep hot on back of grill). Put 2 table-spoons butter in skillet and heat until it bubbles. Stir in almonds, parsley and lemon juice. Pour over fish. Start charcoal about 30 minutes before frying fish.

BACON-STUFFED TROUT

2 eggs
1 T. cream or milk
1 tsp. dried parsley flakes
1 clove garlic, minced

½ tsp. allspice
8 cleaned brook trout
8 or 16 strips of grilled bacon

Beat first 5 ingredients. Coat fish inside and out with egg mixture. Put 1 or 2 strips bacon in each trout and place in greased wire broil basket or on greased hot grill. Cook over hot coals 20 minutes or until fish flakes when tested with fork. Turn once. Serves 8.

HERBED FISH

1-1½ to 2 lb. fish (whitefish
   trout or fresh water fish)
½ C. butter
1 tsp. salt and dash pepper
1 tsp. coriander seed,
   crushed

¼ tsp. cardamon
2 T. lemon juice
1 C. yogurt
Fresh fennel, dill or other
   leafy herbs

Salt fish. Melt butter. Mix in seasonings, lemon juice and yogurt. Coat fish inside and out with mixture. Place in wire broil basket and cook over coals until fish browns on both sides and flakes when tested with a fork, about 25 to 30 minutes. Brush often with sauce. Ten minutes before end of cooking time, make a bed of leafy herbs on grill top. Lay fish atop. Grill until herbs smolder and flavor the fish. Turn once. Serves 4 to 6.

FISH CROUQUETTES

2 C. flaked, cooked fish,
such as salmon, canned
may be used

2 eggs
1 T. finely chopped parsley
1 T. finely chopped onion

Mix fish, eggs, onions and parsley. Roll into cylindrical croquettes or cakes. Then roll in fine cracker crumbs. In heavy skillet over medium coals, melt small amount of shortening. Then add croquettes and brown on all sides.

SPIT BARBECUED WHOLE FISH

Select a 4 to 6 pound fresh or thawed salmon, red snapper, whitefish, lake trout, pike or other whole fish. Wash and pat dry. Brush cavity with lemon juice and sprinkle with salt and pepper. Close cavity with small skewers laced with heavy oiled string. Insert rotisserie spit the length of the fish next to backbone. Brush well with oil or melted butter or margarine. Cook fish 50 to 60 minutes over medium coals. Meat will flake easily when tested. Allow ½ pound raw fish per person. Serve with Coral Sauce.

CORAL SAUCE: Combine and mix ¾ cup mayonnaise, ¼ cup catsup, 2 teaspoons finely chopped pimento, 2 teaspoons lemon juice, 1 teaspoon horseradish and ½ teaspoon paprika. Chill. Yields 1 cup.

HICKORY FISH BAKE

6 fish fillets,
 ¾ to 1" thick
2 or 3 lemons, thinly sliced

½ C. butter or margarine,
 melted
1 or 2 cloves garlic, minced

Sprinkle fish with salt and pepper. Arrange half the lemon slices on bottom of a shallow baking dish. Add fish in single layer. Place remaining lemon slices atop. Combine butter and garlic. Pour over fish and use for basting later. Add hickory to slow coals. Place baking dish on heavy-duty foil on top of grill. Close hood. Cook slowly about 1 hour, turning once. Baste frequently. Serve with lemon slices and butter. Serves 6.

FISH STICKS IN A BASKET

Dip frozen breaded fish sticks (8 ounce package) quickly into ¼ cup melted butter or margarine and 2 tablespoons lemon juice. Place fish sticks in wire broiler and cook over hot coals, brushing with lemon butter, turning once. Broil about 5 minutes. Sticks will brown nicely. Split and toast 5 coney buns. Spread hot buns with sandwich spread. Serve 2 fish sticks on each bun. Serves 5.

FISH IN CORN HUSKS

In the cavity of each cleaned fish, place a 1" pat of butter and give fish a generous squirt of lemon juice. Sprinkle with salt and fresh ground pepper. Wrap each in a whole desilked corn husk. (If husks are dry, soak in water 5 minutes.) Tie with string. Place on bed of hot coals; top with more coals. Cook about 15 minutes or until fish flakes when tested with fork.

FISH AND BACON VARIATION: Sprinkle fish cavity with salt and pepper. Place a bacon strip down each side of the fish. Wrap in husks and cook as above.

HICKORY SMOKED TURKEY

1-10 lb. ready-to-cook turkey
¼ C. salad oil
¼ C. salt

1 C. vinegar
¼ C. pepper
2 tsp. parsley, finely
  chopped

Rinse bird and pat dry. Make a paste of oil and salt. Rub ¼ cup of mixture inside the bird. Truss turkey and balance on spit or use rotary roast rack. brush with salad oil. Have slow coals at back of barbecue, a drip pan under revolving bird. For moisture, place a pan of water at end of firebox. Roast, hood down, for 1 hour. Then brush with sauce made by combining the remaining salt with vinegar, pepper and parsley. Place damp hickory chips on coals. Roast, hood down, 3½ to 4 hours longer. Baste bird every 30 minutes. Let rest about 15 minutes before carving.

ROTISSERIE TURKEY

10 to 12 lb. turkey
½ C. melted butter

½ tsp. prepared poultry
seasoning

Rub salt inside bird. Truss turkey securely. Balance on rotisserie spit. Cook over medium coals, 4½ to 5 hours with lid closed. Baste often with seasoned butter. Allow ½ pound ready to cook turkey per person.

SPITTED BREAST OF TURKEY

One turkey breast, 5 to 8 pounds. Rub well with butter and tie in a compact form, spitting it through the center. Roast over moderate coals, basting with olive oil and vermouth or butter and white wine. A 6-pound turkey will take 1½ to 2½ hours. Do not overcook.

TURKEY THIGHS

The thighs will weigh about 1½ pounds each. Remove bone from the thighs. Lard them with strips of salt pork, then roll and tie in a compact form. Spit and roast, basting while cooking. This will take 1½ to 2 hours over medium coals.

TURKEY LEGS

Use legs ¾ to 1 pound each. Spread with softened butter and lay on grill, skin side up. Cook over medium heat, about 1½ hours, turning occasionally and basting with white wine and melted butter to which dill, tarragon, curry or rosemary has been added.

ROCK CORNISH HENS
(SPIT BARBECUED)

4 thawed Cornish hens,
  ¾ to 1¼ lbs. each
1 tsp. salt
Barbecue Sauce

Wild rice stuffing, optional
⅓ C. melted butter or
  margarine or a flavored
  butter spread

Clean, rinse and pat dry the hens. Season cavity with salt and stuffing if desired. Fasten neck skin to back with small metal skewers. Close lower body cavity of bird, if stuffed, by using small metal skewers and lacing string. Flatten wings against breast by tying securely with light cord. Push spit lengthwise through bird, starting at neck. Balance hens on spit so motor will work smoothly. Brush hens with melted butter. Attach spit and start motor. Cook over medium-high coals (375°) at spit level, about 45 minutes to 1¼ hours or until leg joint moves easily.

WILD RICE STUFFING: Melt ⅓ cup butter in pan. Add ¾ cup diced celery and ½ cup sliced green onion. Cook slowly until tender, not brown. Add 1 teaspoon salt, 1 can (4 ounces) mushroom pieces, chopped, 2 cups cooked long grain rice, 1 package (4 ounces) wild rice, cooked and drained. Toss lightly.

BACONY BUTTER OR BASTING SAUCE: Stir ½ cup crisp bacon bits, 2 teaspoons minced parsley and ¼ teaspoon liquid smoke in 1 cup butter or margarine. Yields 1⅓ cups.

NO-WATCH ROASTED CHICKEN
(PIECES OR QUARTERS)

Brush chicken pieces generously with cooking oil, melted butter or margarine. Season with salt and pepper. Arrange in well-greased flat spit basket. Clamp on cover and run spit through basket. Attach to spit motor as manufacturer suggests. Start motor and cook over medium to medium-high heat until well browned and fork-tender, 30 to 50 minutes, depending on size of pieces. Baste every 15 minutes while cooking.

CHICKEN

Salt cavities of whole broiler-fryer chickens (about 2 to 2½ pounds each). Mount birds on spit. Attach spit to rotisserie and turn on motor. Use medium coals, with a drip pan under birds. Baste chicken often with a mixture of ½ cup cooking oil and ¼ cup lemon juice. The last 30 minutes brush often with Basting Sauce. Allow 2 hours roasting time without barbecue hood, 1¾ hours with hood down.

BASTING SAUCE:
¼ C. cooking oil
¼ C. dry white wine
¼ C. chicken broth
2 T. lemon juice
2 T. apple jelly
1 tsp. salt

1 tsp. snipped parsley
½ tsp. prepared mustard
¼ tsp. Worcestershire sauce
Dash of celery seed
Rosemary
Pepper

Combine all above ingredients. Beat smooth. 105

BROILED CHICKEN

¼ C. salad oil
¼ C. cooking wine
¼ C. chicken broth
2 T. lemon juice
2 T. apple jelly
1 tsp. salt

½ tsp. monosodium
 glutamate
1 tsp. snipped parsley
½ tsp. prepared mustard
½ tsp. Worcestershire sauce
Dash of celery seed,
 rosemary and pepper

2 broilers (2 to 2½ lbs. each), halved lengthwise

Combine all ingredients except chicken. Whip out lumps of jelly with beater. Brush chicken with the sauce and place bone side down on grill. Broil over slow coals, turning occasionally and basting often, about 1 hour or until meat is tender and skin is crisp and dark. Serves 4.

MARINATED DRUMSTICKS

¼ C. catsup
2 to 3 T. lemon juice
2 T. soy sauce

¼ C. cooking oil
12 chicken drumsticks

Combine all ingredients except chicken legs; mix well. Add chicken legs and turn to cover. Place in refrigerator overnight. Spoon marinade over once in awhile. Place drumsticks in wire broiler basket. Broil over medium coals for about 1 hour or until tender. Turn occasionally and baste with marinade. Serves 6.

CHARCOAL-BROILED CHICKEN BREASTS

Allow 1 chicken breast per person. Marinate for 3 hours in ¼ cup melted butter, ¼ cup soy sauce and ¼ cup white wine, 1 teaspoon tarragon and 1 teaspoon dry mustard. Broil over charcoal 10 minutes or until tender and juicy. Baste often with marinade.

STUFFED BROILED CHICKEN BREASTS

Cut small pockets in the breasts. Make a paste with ⅛ pound butter, ¼ cup each chopped parsley, chives or green onions, 1 teaspoon dried basil. Stuff the chicken with this mixture and secure with toothpicks. Brush each breast with butter. Broil over medium coals for 10 to 12 minutes, starting on the bone side and finishing skin side down. A few minutes before they are done, brush them with heavy cream and sprinkle with salt and pepper.

BROILED CHICKEN HEARTS

Marinate one pound chicken hearts in equal parts soy sauce, oil and sherry. Add a little garlic if you wish. String on skewers and broil for about 4 minutes on each side. They will be brown and crispy.

VEGETABLES

ROTISSERIE VEGETABLES

Roast vegetables whole, each kind on a separate spit so you can start or stop cooking at the right time. Choose whatever vegetables you want to serve; potatoes, onions, squash (zucchini or acorn), eggplant, sweet potatoes, tomatoes, green or red peppers, turnips. Wash vegetables, leaving jackets on. Brush with melted butter or salad oil. Let turn over coals until done, basting once in awhile with butter. Tomatoes cook in a very short time. Sweet potatoes 20 to 45 minutes, turnips 25 top 30 minutes, baking potatoes and acorn squash need 45 minutes to an hour. If they are done too early, wrap in foil and keep warm on side of grill.

RANCH STYLE ONIONS

Melt butter or margarine in skillet or foilware pan on grill. Add ½" slices of onion in single layer. Salt. Cook slowly over coals until golden, turning often.

SMOKY BAKED BEANS

4 oz. salt pork, cut in
½" cubes
2-1 lb. cans pork and beans

½ C. catsup
¼ C. brown sugar
1 tsp. dry mustard

Brown pork in skillet; drain. In a 2-quart bean pot, combine remaining ingredients. Top with pork. Bake uncovered on grill over medium coals with hood down 1 hour or longer. For smoke flavor, toss piece of damp hickory on coals while beans are cooking. Serves 8.

LIMA BEAN SUPREME

1 lb. large dry limas
2 C. chopped onions
½ C. sliced mushrooms

2 T. paprika
2 C. dairy sour cream
1 tsp. salt

Place rinsed beans in pan with 6 cups cold water. Bring to boil. Simmer 2 minutes. Remove from heat and let stand 1 hour, covered. Add 2 teaspoons salt to beans and liquid. Place pan on grill. Bring to a boil. Move to side of grill. Cover and simmer 45 to 60 minutes or until tender. In large skillet on grill, cook onions in ¼ cup butter until tender. Add mushrooms and paprika. Cook 5 minutes. Stir in beans, sour cream and salt. Serves 12.

PARMESAN POTATOES

Scrub 3 large baking potatoes. Cut in ¼" lengthwise slices. Spread out on a 20" length of 18" wide foil. Sprinkle with onion salt, celery salt and freshly ground black pepper. Sprinkle with ⅓ cup grated parmesan cheese. Now overlap potato slices and dot with butter. Bring edges of foil together, leaving a little space for steam. Seal well. Place wrapped potatoes on grill. Cook over coals 30 to 45 minutes or until done, turning several times.

POTATO PANCAKES

1½ C. raw potatoes, peeled
  grated, patted dry
1 tsp. salt
1 tsp. baking powder

2 T. flour
1 egg, optional
Canned milk

Mix all ingredients, adding only enough milk to bind the mixture. Add ½ cup minced onions, if desired. Drop by spoonfuls onto a well-greased griddle over medium-high coals, 4 to 6" over heat. Turn only once when the bottom is golden brown.

CHEESY POTATOES IN FOIL

3 large baking potatoes,
  peeled and salted
Coarse ground pepper
4 or 5 slices bacon,
  crisp, cooked

1 large onion, sliced
8 oz. sharp process
  American cheese, cubed
½ C. butter or margarine

Slice potatoes in a large piece of heavy aluminum foil. Season with salt and pepper. Crumble bacon on top. Add onions and cheese. Slice butter or all. Bring edges of foil up, leaving space for expansion of steam. Seal well. Lay on grill and cook over coals for 1 hour or until done. Turn several times or cook on grill with barbecue hood down, 45 minutes. Serves 4 to 6.

SKILLET POTATOES

4 C. cooked, diced potatoes
2 C. sliced onions
2 T. snipped parsley
2 T. chopped pimento

½ tsp. salt
¼ tsp. pepper
¼ C. shortening

Combine potatoes, onions, parsley, pimento, salt and pepper in skillet with hot fat. Brown on top of grill until golden brown and crisp. Serves 6.

ONIONED POTATOES

6 medium baking potatoes   1 env. onion soup mix
½ C. soft butter or
  margarine

Scrub potatoes. Cut each in 3 or 4 lengthwise slices. Blend butter and soup mix. Spread on slices. Put on squares of foil and wrap tightly. Bake until done, turning once, on the grill or right on top of coals, 45 to 60 minutes. Serves 6.

GRILLED AU GRATIN POTATOES

3 C. unpeeled thinly sliced
  potatoes
1 C. thinly sliced onion

6 to 8 slices process
  American cheese
1 tsp. salt
Dash of pepper

Arrange alternate layers of sliced potatoes, onions and cheese on 18x14" piece of heavy-duty foil. Sprinkle with salt and pepper. Fold foil into tight package. Place on medium coals for 45 minutes or until done. Turn every 15 minutes. Serves 4.

FOILED POTATOES

Scrub medium baking potatoes. Brush with salad oil. Wrap each in a piece of foil. Bake 45 to 60 minutes on the grill or right on top of coals. Turn occasionally.

HERB FRENCH FRIES

2 pkgs. frozen French fries *½ tsp. herbs*
Salt and pepper *Quilted foil*

Place frozen potatoes in foil. Add salt, pepper and herbs. Wrap in foil and place on grill, turning occasionally, until done, about 8 minutes. Serves 4.

TOMATOES WITH CHEESE

4 large ripe tomatoes
Salt and pepper
¼ C. soft bread crumbs

1 oz. sharp American
  cheese, shredded
1 T. butter or margarine,
  melted
Snipped parsley

Slice off tops of tomatoes. Season with salt and pepper. Combine bread crumbs, cheese and butter. Sprinkle over tomatoes. Garnish with parsley. Place in foilware pan and grill on medium-hot coals about 20 minutes or until heated through. Serve immediately. Serves 4.

GRILL TOP TOMATOES

Cut tomatoes in half. Brush cut surfaces with Italian salad dressing. Sprinkle with salt, pepper and basil. Place cut side up on foil or greased grill over hot coals, about 10 minutes or until hot. Don't turn.

STUFFED GREEN PEPPERS

In a large heavy skillet, place large peppers which have been washed. Have the tops cut off and the insides scooped out. Stuff each one with beef hash or hamburger mixture. Set each pepper in skillet. Add ¼" of water. Cover the skillet and cook over medium coals about 20 minutes.

PEAS IN FOIL

1 pkg. frozen peas
2 T. onion soup mix

2 T. butter
2 T. crisp chopped bacon

Blend the onion, butter and bacon. Take the peas out of package and mix them with the butter mixture. Wrap the peas in foil and cook on grill over medium heat 15 minutes.

INDIAN-STYLE CORN ON THE COB

Turn back husks and strip off silk. Lay husks back in position. Place ears on grill over hot coals, Roast, turning often, 15 to 20 minutes or until husks are dry and brown. Serve with special butter.

ZIPPY BUTTER: Soften ½ cup butter or margarine. Add 1 tablespoon salt, dash of pepper. Blend until fluffy.

HERB BUTTER: Soften ½ cup butter or margarine. Add ½ teaspoon dried rosemary, crushed and ½ teaspoon dried marjoram, crushed. Blend until fluffy.

CORN ON THE COB

Remove husks from fresh corn. Remove silk with stiff brush. Place each ear on aluminum foil. Spread each ear with soft butter. Sprinkle with salt and pepper. Wrap in foil, don't seal seams, but fold or twist foil around ends. Roast over hot coals, 15 to 20 minutes. Turn ears often. Serve with special butter.

GRILLED CORN ON THE COB

¼ lb. soft butter or
  margarine
1 T. soy sauce

½ tsp. tarragon leaves
6 ears fresh corn

Blend butter, soy sauce and tarragon leaves. Husk corn. Lay each ear on piece of foil large enough to wrap around it. Spread each ear with seasoned butter. Wrap corn and seal edges. Cook on grill 3" from coals 20 to 30 minutes. Turn often. Serves 6.

NOTES • NOTES • NOTES • NOTES • NOTES

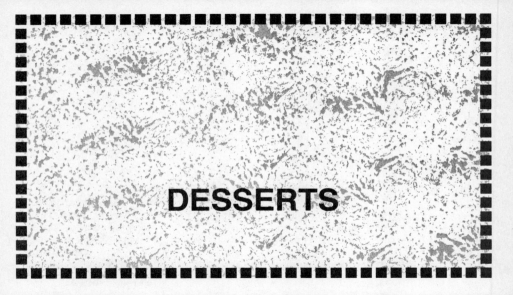

DESSERTS

FLAMING PEACHES OR PEARS

At about serving time, heat ¼ cup each of butter or margarine, brown sugar and canned peach or pear syrup in heavy (10") frypan. Place over medium grill, 5 to 7" from heat until syrup is bubbly, stirring constantly. Add 8 small well-drained peach or pear halves and 8 maraschino cherries. Spoon syrup over fruit until it is well glazed and hot. Move skillet to a cooler spot on grill to slow glazing. Pour ¼ cup brandy or cognac over fruit. Touch a lighted match to edge of liquid. Serve plain, on pound cake slices or ice cream, when flame dies. Serves 4 to 6.

FRUIT COBBLER

1-12 oz. pkg. frozen, sliced
  peaches
1-10 oz. pkg. frozen red
  raspberries
1½ C. prepared biscuit mix

¼ C. sugar
3 T. oil or melted and cooled
  butter
⅓ C. milk (or enough to
  make a soft dough)

Combine partially defrosted fruit and add 3 tablespoons butter in large (10") heavy frypan with fireproof handle. Cover and place to one side of medium grill, 4 to 6" from heat. Bring to a simmer. While fruit is heating, combine 1½ cups prepared biscuit mix, ¼ cup sugar, 3 tablespoons oil or melted and cooled butter. Add ⅓ cup milk (or enough to make a soft dough). Drop 6 to 8 spoonfuls of dough into hot bubbly fruit. Cover. Pull pan to cool side of grill. Cook until dough is done, 12 to 15 minutes. Sprinkle top with cinnamon and sugar. Yields 6 to 8 servings.

FRUIT DESSERT KABOBS

Have bowls of 1½" banana slices, bite-size chunks of fresh pineapple, watermelon pickle slices, unpeeled red plum halves, peeled orange wedges and Curried Orange Sauce around a small grill. Let each person thread their own skewer. Barbecue over medium grill 4 to 5" from heat until bananas are golden brown and fruit is warm.

CURRIED ORANGE SAUCE: Combine ¼ cup sugar, 2 teaspoons cornstarch, ¼ teaspoon curry powder, 1½ teaspoons grated orange rind and ¼ teaspoon salt. Stir in 1 cup orange juice and 1 tablespoon lemon juice. Cook, stirring constantly, until thickened. Yields 1 cup.

GRILLED GRAPEFRUIT

Cut grapefruit in half crosswise. Remove seeds and loosen fruit from membrane. Sprinkle surface with sugar and a bit of sherry, grenadine syrup or creme de menthe. Center each grapefruit half on a double piece of foil. Wrap loosely but secure. Place cut surface up on medium grill, 5 to 7" from heat and allow to warm, 10 to 15 minutes.

CINNAMON APPLE SLICES

Slice 4 medium, peeled and cored apples crosswise into 4 rings each. Cut 8 double thick 8" squares of heavy foil. Center 2 apple rings on each square. Pour ½ teaspoon water into each cavity. Sprinkle slices with 2 teaspoons sugar and a dash of cinnamon. Dot with 1 teaspoon butter. Sprinkle 1 teaspoon raisins and nuts, if desired. Seal package. Place folded side up on grill, about 4" above medium coals, 30 to 40 minutes. This goes well with pork, ham, beef or poultry. Serves 8.

GRILLED BANANAS

Combine ¼ cup melted butter, 1 tablespoon each lemon or orange juice and honey and a dash of salt. Mix well. Cut 8 double thick 12" squares of heavy foil. Center a peeled banana on foil, fold edges of foil up around banana. Brush the bananas with an equal amount of the butter mixture. Sprinkle each with 2 teaspoons flaked coconut. Fold foil around banana securely. Place fold side up, on medium hibachi or small grill, 4 to 6" from coals, 12 to 15 minutes. This can be used as a dessert or with meat. Yields 8 servings.

BANANA SHORTCAKE

¼ C. butter
2 or 3 green-tipped bananas,
  peeled and quartered
2 T. lemon juice

⅔ C. brown sugar
¼ tsp. cinnamon
4-1" slices pound cake
Sour cream

Melt butter in foilware pan over hot coals. Add bananas, drizzle with lemon juice, brown sugar and cinnamon. Cook until bananas are just soft, spooning syrup over once in awhile. Toast cake slices on the grill on both sides. Spoon bananas over warm cake slices. Top with sour cream.

CAKE KABOBS

Cut a pound cake or angel cake in 1½" cubes. Spear each on fork and dip in melted currant jelly or in sweetened condensed milk. Then roll in flaked coconut to cover. String on skewers and toast over very hot coals, turning often.

GRILL-BAKED CAKE

Prepare 1 package pudding cake mix (your favorite flavor) according to package directions, but using an ungreased 8½x1½" round foil pan. Place on grill top over hot coals; lower hood to make oven. Bake 25 to 30 minutes. Prepared cake just before ready to bake. Spoon servings while warm, turning pudding side up. Good with ice cream. This dessert will bake while you are eating.

S'MORES

Toast marshmallows over coals. For each treat have a graham cracker covered with a square of milk chocolate. Slip 2 browned marshmallows atop. Add graham cracker lid, then squash down.

POW WOW SUNDAE

String ¼ pound marshmallows on skewers. Toast over coals until melty inside and browned. Take off skewers. Put into 1 cup chocolate syrup. Stir just to marble, then ladle over big scoops of vanilla ice cream.

MISCELLANEOUS

BARBECUED BREAD

1 round pumpernickel loaf
½ C. soft butter
2 T. prepared mustard

½ C. grated Parmesan
  cheese
¼ C. snipped parsley

Cut bread in ½" slices. Mix remaining ingredients. Spread over slices. Put loaf on large piece of foil. Cut loaf in half lengthwise, going almost to bottom crust. Seal bread in foil and heat at side of grill 20 to 25 minutes. Turn occasionally.

ONION CHEESE LOAF

Cut French bread in 1" slices, cutting to, but not through bottom of loaf. Combine ⅓ cup butter, softened, and 3 tablespoons prepared mustard. Spread over cut surfaces of bread. Insert slices of sharp process American cheese and thin slices of onion in slashes. Wrap loaf in foil; heat over medium coals about 15 minutes or until hot through.

ROLL ON A SPIT

Thread brown and serve rolls on a spit. Brush all sides with melted butter. Rotate over coals 10 to 15 minutes.

BUTTER BISCUITS

Brush top and bottom of 1 package (8 ounces) refrigerated biscuits with soft butter or margarine. Arrange biscuits on a dcuble thick 18" square heavy foil. Fold over biscuits, seal leaving space for biscuits to rise. Place to one side of grill over medium heat, 6 to 8" above heat. Bake 6 to 7 minutes. Turn package. Brown second side 5 to 7 minutes Yields 10 rolls.

TEXAS CAKES

1 C. packaged biscuit mix
16 oz. can evaporated milk

½ of 1 lb. can (¾ C.)
canned beans with chili
gravy

Beat biscuit mix and milk until smooth. Stir in beans. Bake on a hot well-greased skillet or griddle on the grill. Turn cakes when bubbles form. Flip once. Makes 8-4" cakes. Serve with melted butter.

PANCAKES

2 C. flour
2 tsp. baking powder
1 tsp. salt
2 T. sugar

6 T. shortening
3 eggs, beaten
1½ C. milk, powdered
  or canned may
  be used

Mix dry ingredients together and blend shortening into flour. Work ingredients until they look like cornmeal. (This mixture can be carried in a plastic container to use camping.) Stir in eggs and enough milk to bring batter to desired consistency. Cook on greased griddle over medium-hot to hot coals until brown, turning once.

FRENCH TOAST

8 slices bread
6 eggs
¼ C. milk

Dash of salt
1 tsp. bacon fat

Remove crusts from bread (day old bread). Beat the eggs with the milk and salt. Soak bread slices in the egg mixture. Add bacon fat to the skillet or grill and get moderately hot over medium high coals. Carefully put the slices in skillet to fry to a golden brown. Serve with butter and maple syrup or jam and jelly.

BULL'S EYE FRIED EGGS

All you need are slices of bread, butter and eggs for this meal. Remove crusts and cut a large circle in each slice, using a can or something similar. Fry these bread rings in a little butter until they are golden brown on one side. Turn the rings over and drop an egg into the hole. Fry slowly over low to medium coals until the eggs are set, turning over once, if desired. You may add a little minced onion or cheese to the egg after it has been put in the bread ring.

DONUT HOLES

Cut refrigerated biscuits (tube biscuits) in thirds, and roll each into a ball. String on skewers, leaving about ½" between balls. Bake over hot coals, turning constantly until browned and completely done, about 7 minutes. At once, push off skewers into melted butter or margarine, then roll in cinnamon-sugar mixture. These are best eaten fresh. Makes 30 donut holes.

BARBECUED RICE

1 1/3 C. packaged precooked rice
1/2 C. extra-hot catsup
1/2 C. cold water
1-3 oz. can (2/3 C.) broiled sliced mushrooms

1/4 C. finely chopped onions
2 T. chopped green pepper
1/2 tsp. salt
2 T. butter or margarine

Tear a 3-foot length of 18" wide foil. Fold in half to make a square. Make a pouch in foil and add all ingredients, except butter. (Add mushroom liquid, too.) Dot with butter. Seal and place on grill over hot coals 15 to 18 minutes. Stir with fork and sprinkle with parsley. Serves 4.

CAMP COFFEE

Camp coffee is best made in an old-fashioned pot on open fire or your grill top. Break 1 egg, crush the shell. Mix with ½ cup of coffee and ½ cup cold water. Have 4 cups of water boiling in the pot. Add the coffee mixture and stir well. Then bring to a boil. Now push to a cooler part of the fire and allow to stand 3 minutes. Then add ½ cup cold water. Let stand another 3 to 4 minutes to settle. For less stout coffee, add 2 more cups of boiling water.

GRILLED GARLIC SLICES

Melt a little butter in shallow pan over grill. Add garlic powder or minced garlic to taste. Toast thick slices of French bread on grill. Butter, if desired. Serve hot.

UNI-Cookbook Categories

1100	Cookies	3400	Low Cholesterol
1200	Casseroles	3500	Chocoholic
1300	Meat Dishes	3700	Cajun
1400	Microwave	3800	Household Hints
1500	Cooking for "2"	6100	Chinese Recipes
1600	Slow Cooking	6400	German Recipes
1700	Low Calorie	6700	Italian Recipes
1900	Pastries & Pies	6800	Irish Recipes
2000	Charcoal Grilling	7000	Mexican Recipes
2100	Hors D'oeuvres	7100	Norwegian Recipes
2200	Beef	7200	Swedish Recipes
2300	Holiday Collections		
2400	Salads & Dressings		
2500	How to Cook Wild Game		
2600	Soups		
3100	Seafood & Fish		
3200	Poultry		
3300	My Own Recipes		

**Available
Titles 1/94**

**Titles change
without notice.**

**G&R
Publishing Co.**
507 Industrial Street
Waverly, IA 50677